Neo Patterns Collection

Vol.02
Nuevo Patterns
Coloring Book for Adults

by Asma Zergui

ISBN-13:
978-1511442923

ISBN-10:
1511442921

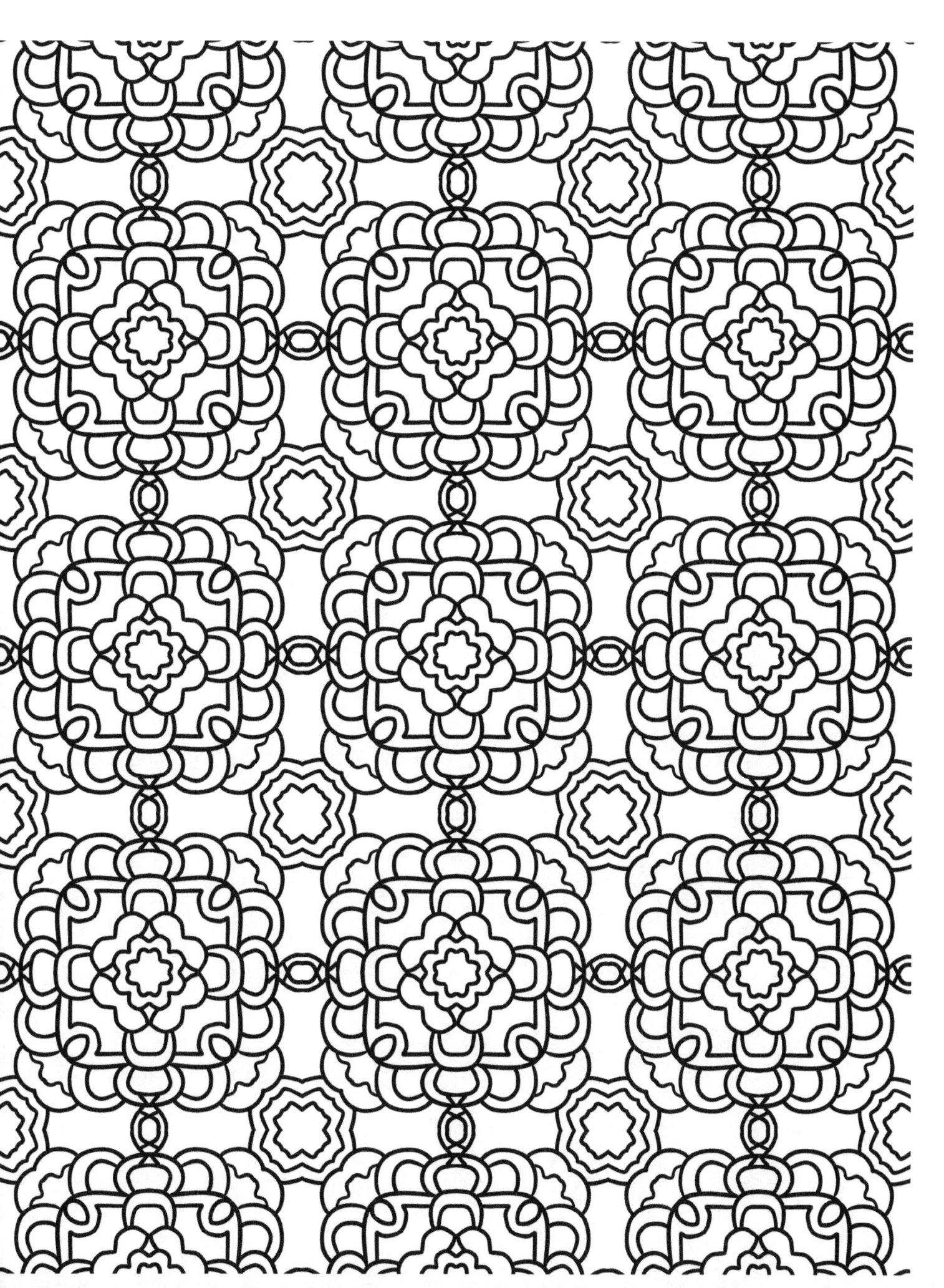

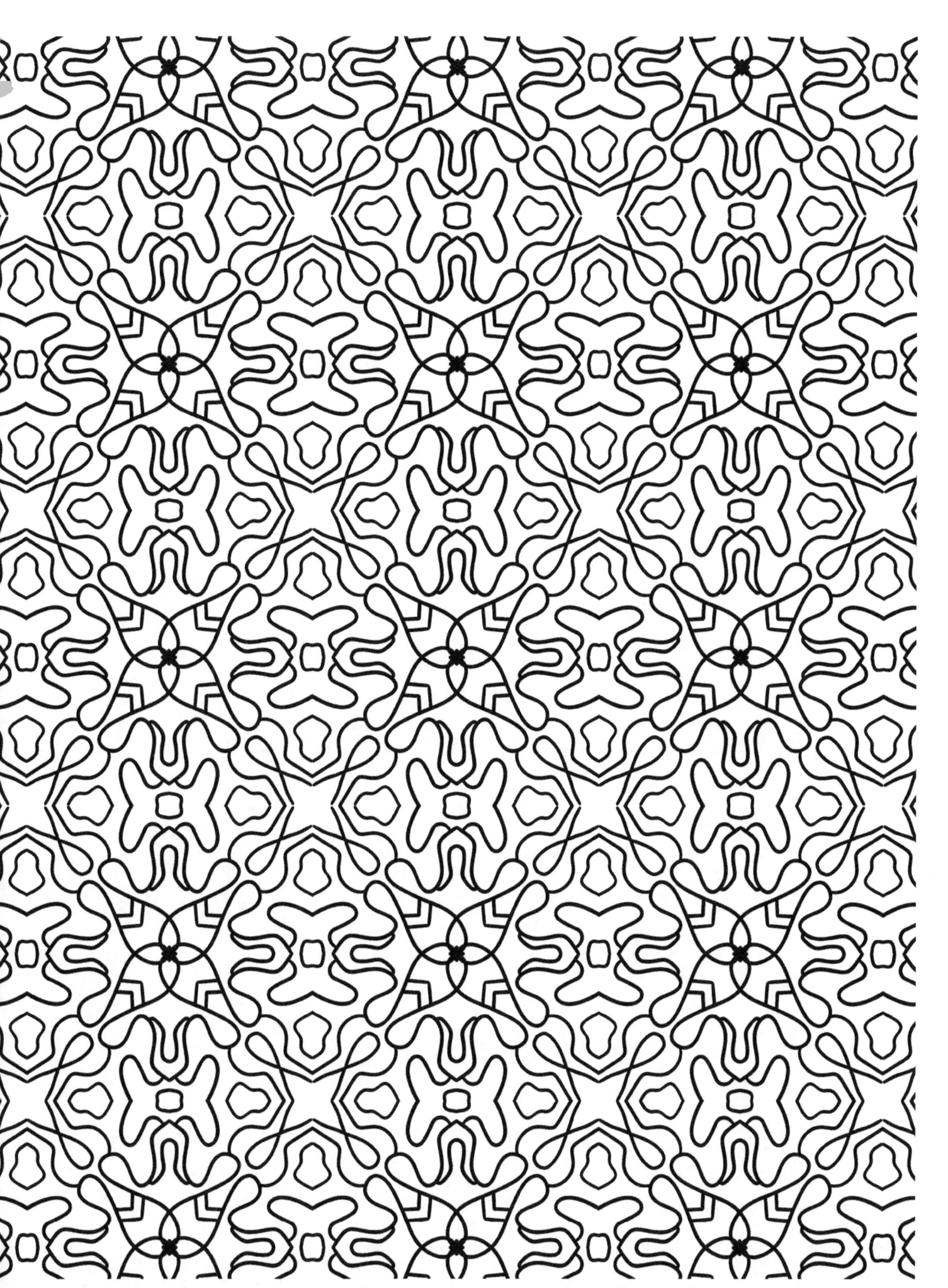

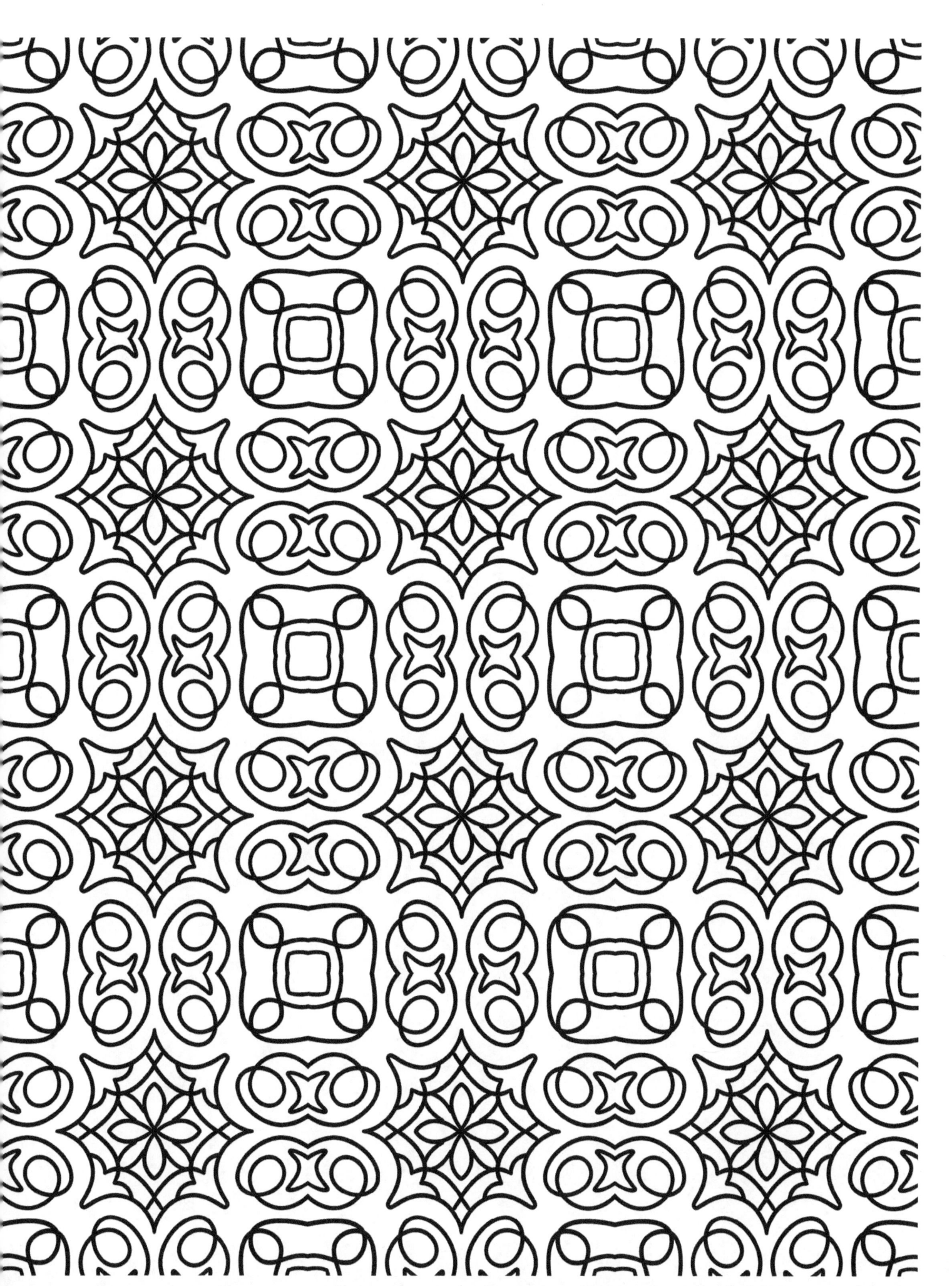

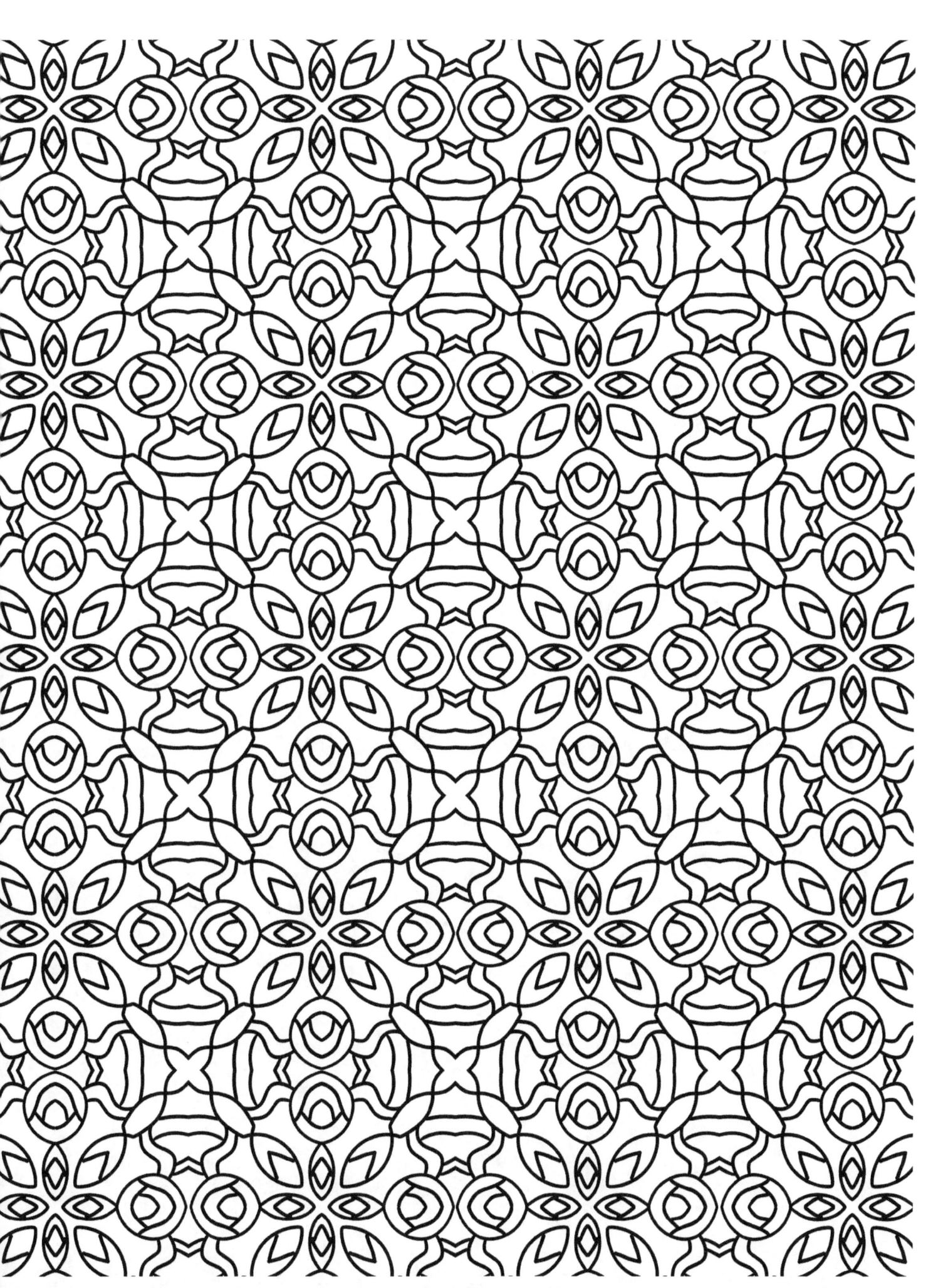

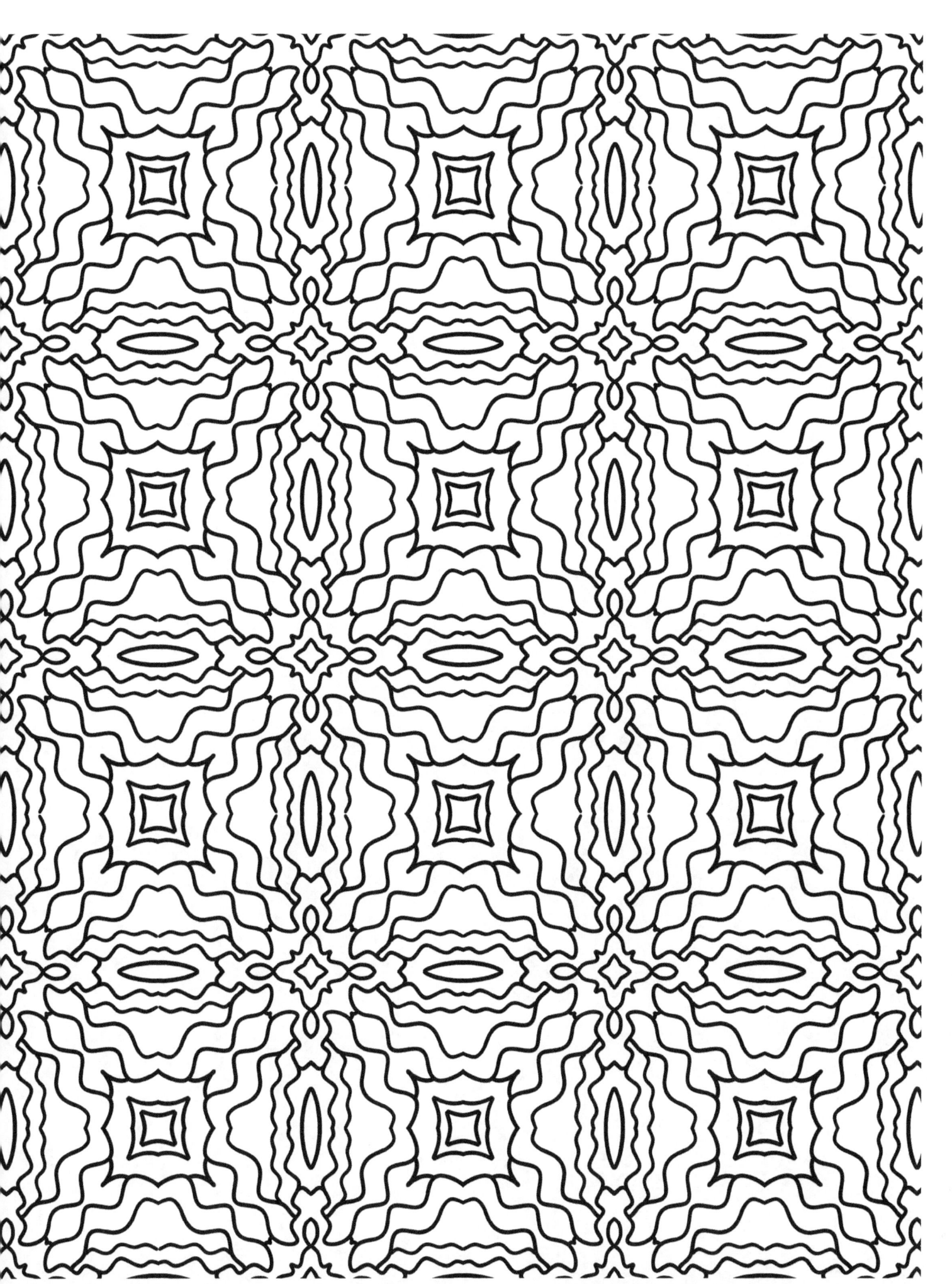

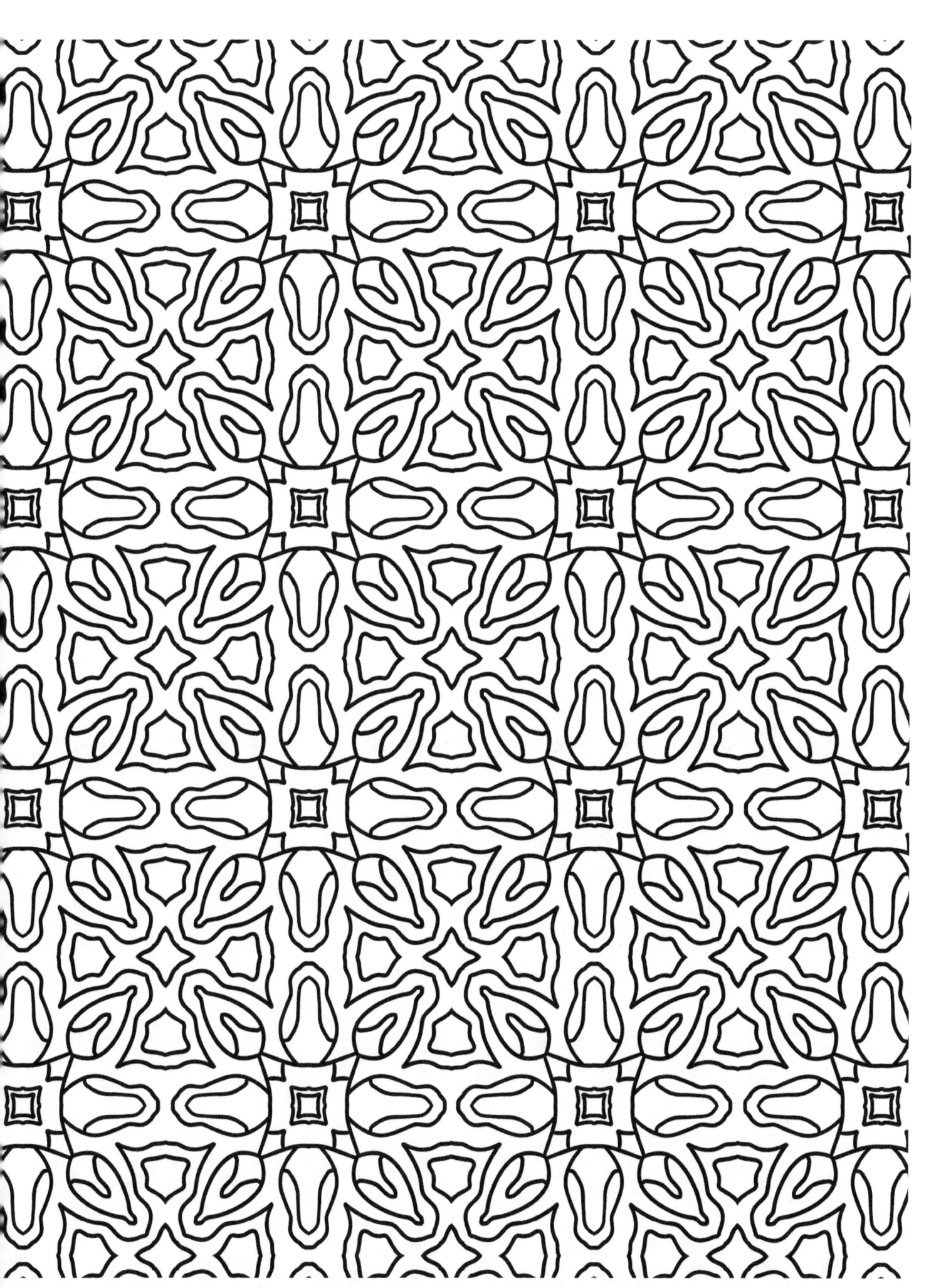

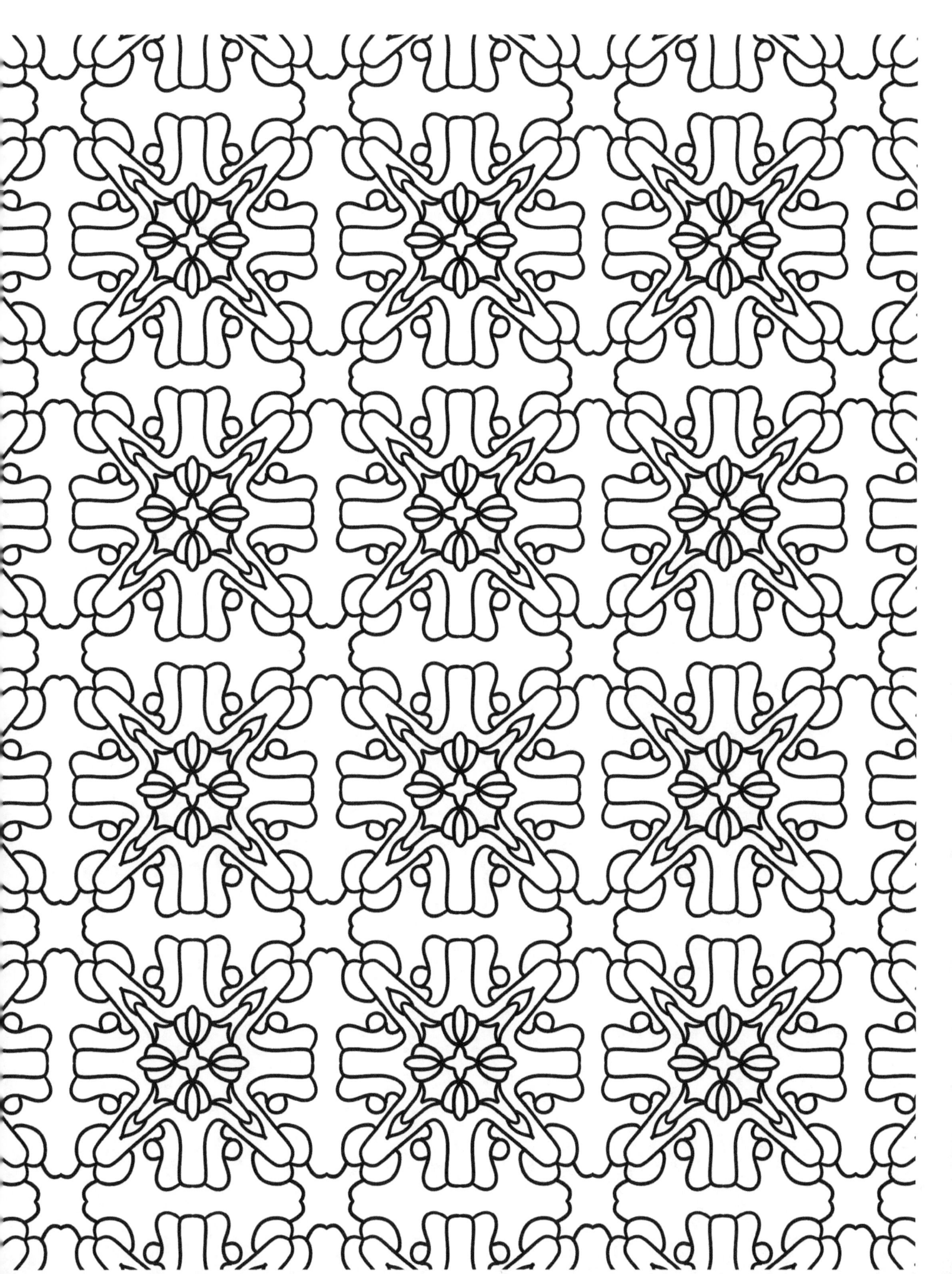

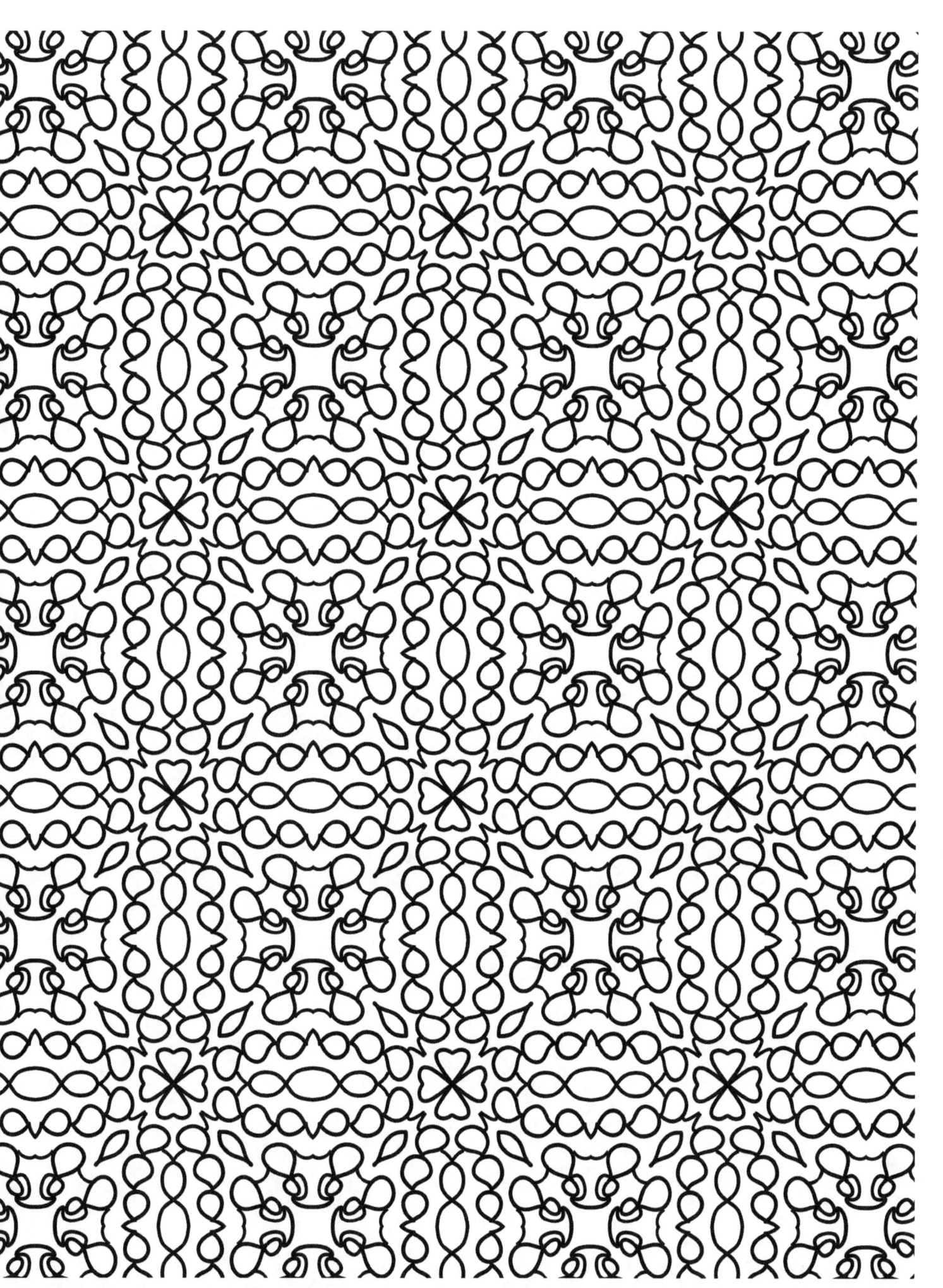

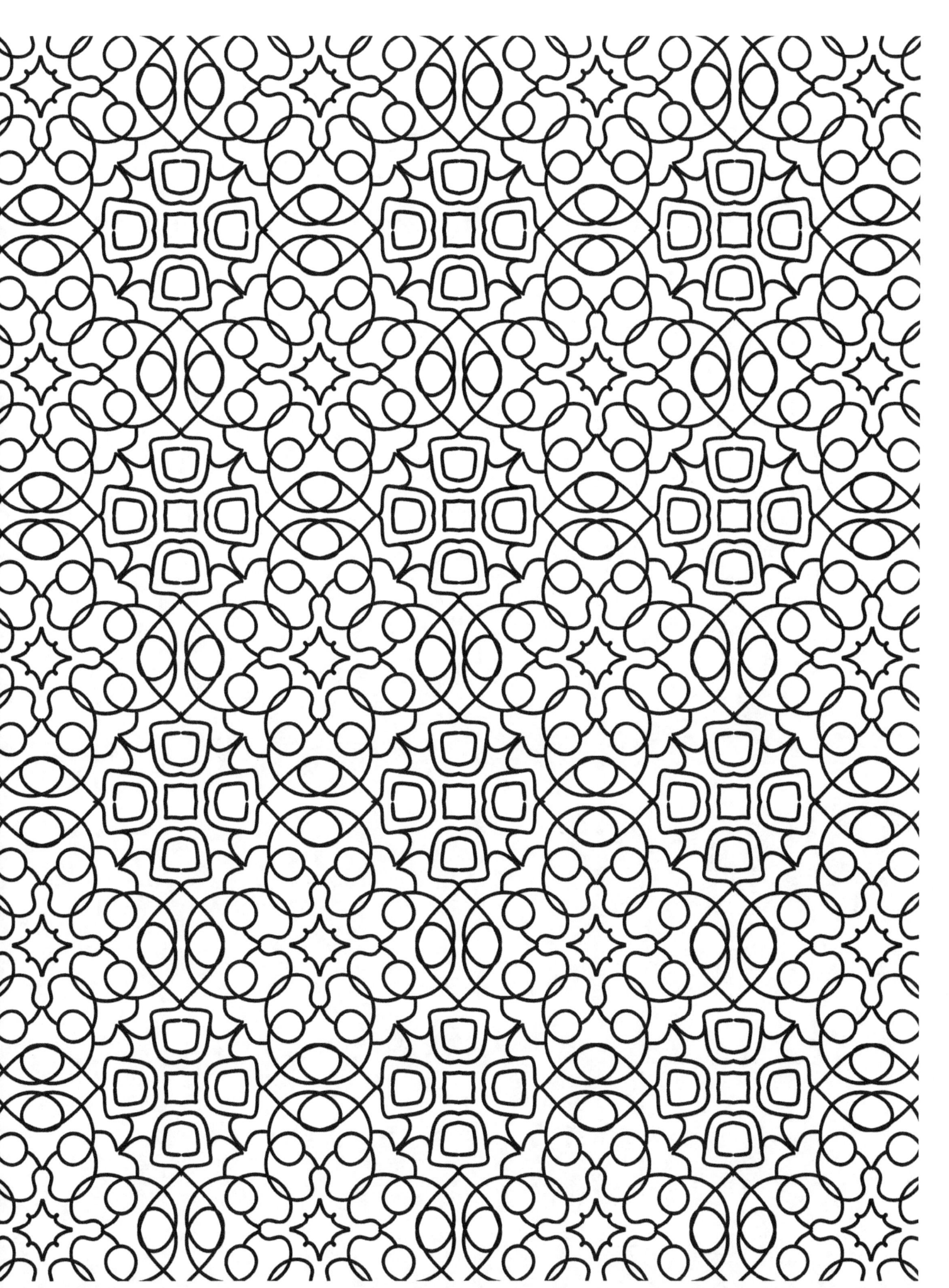

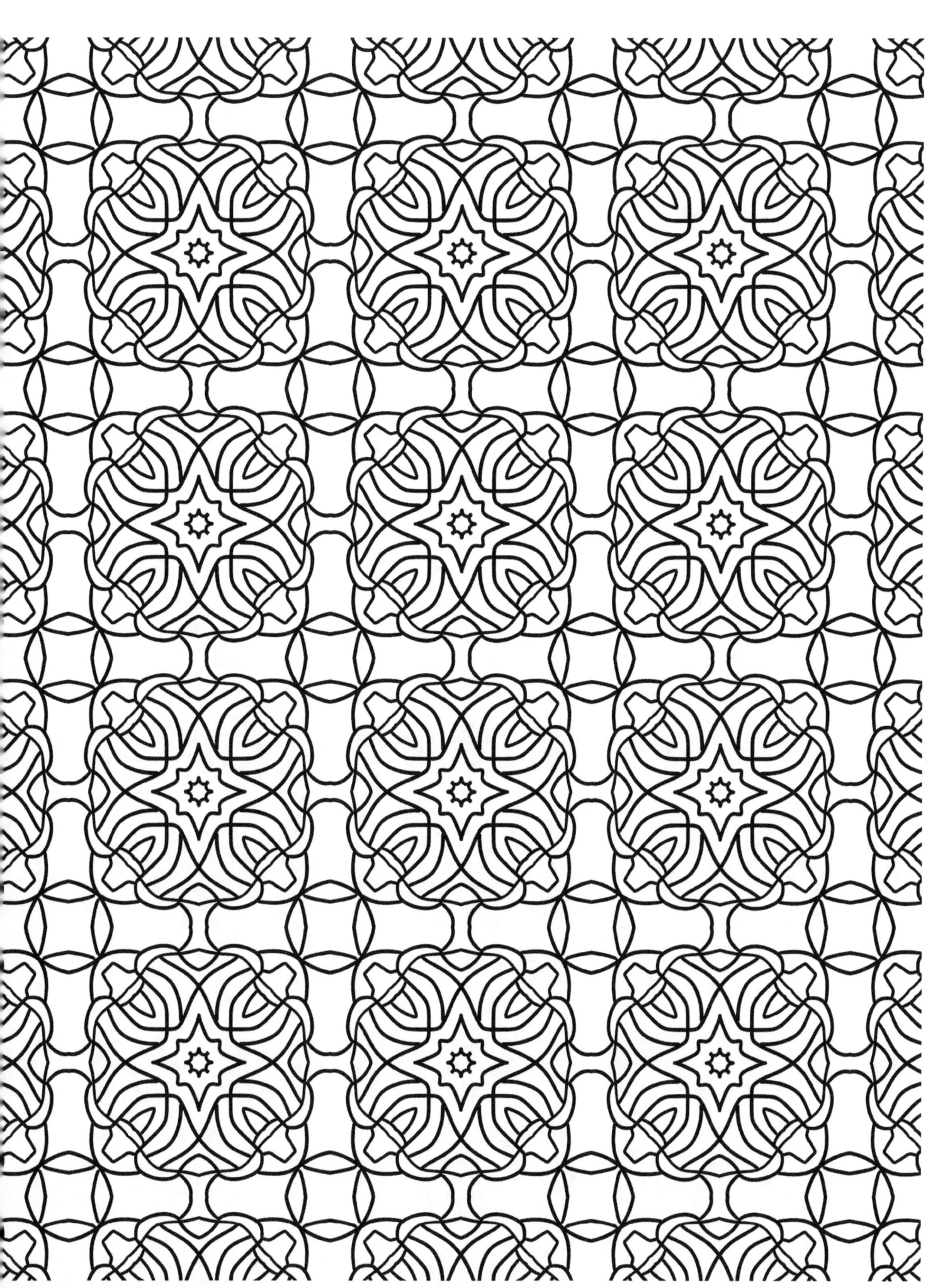

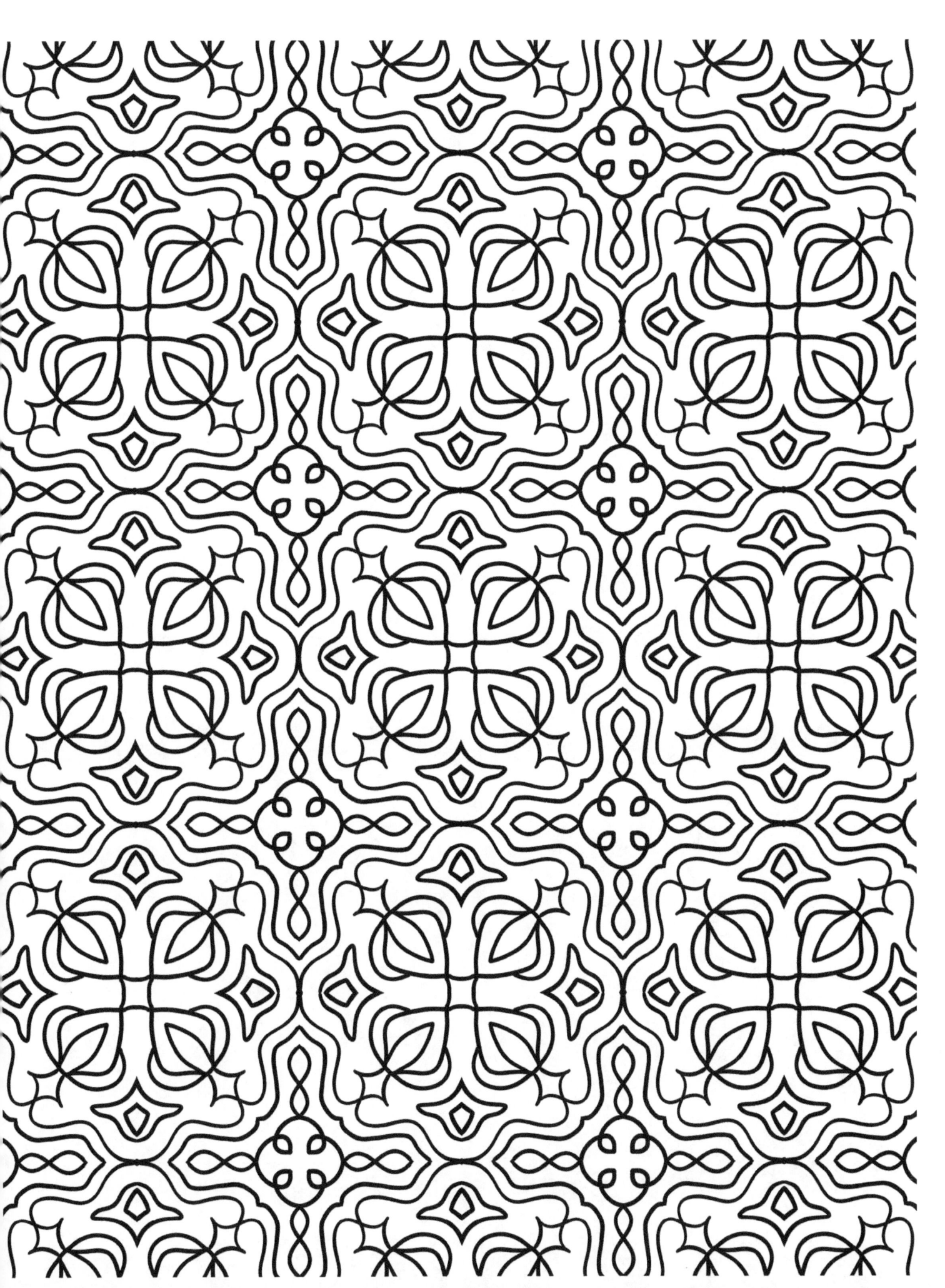

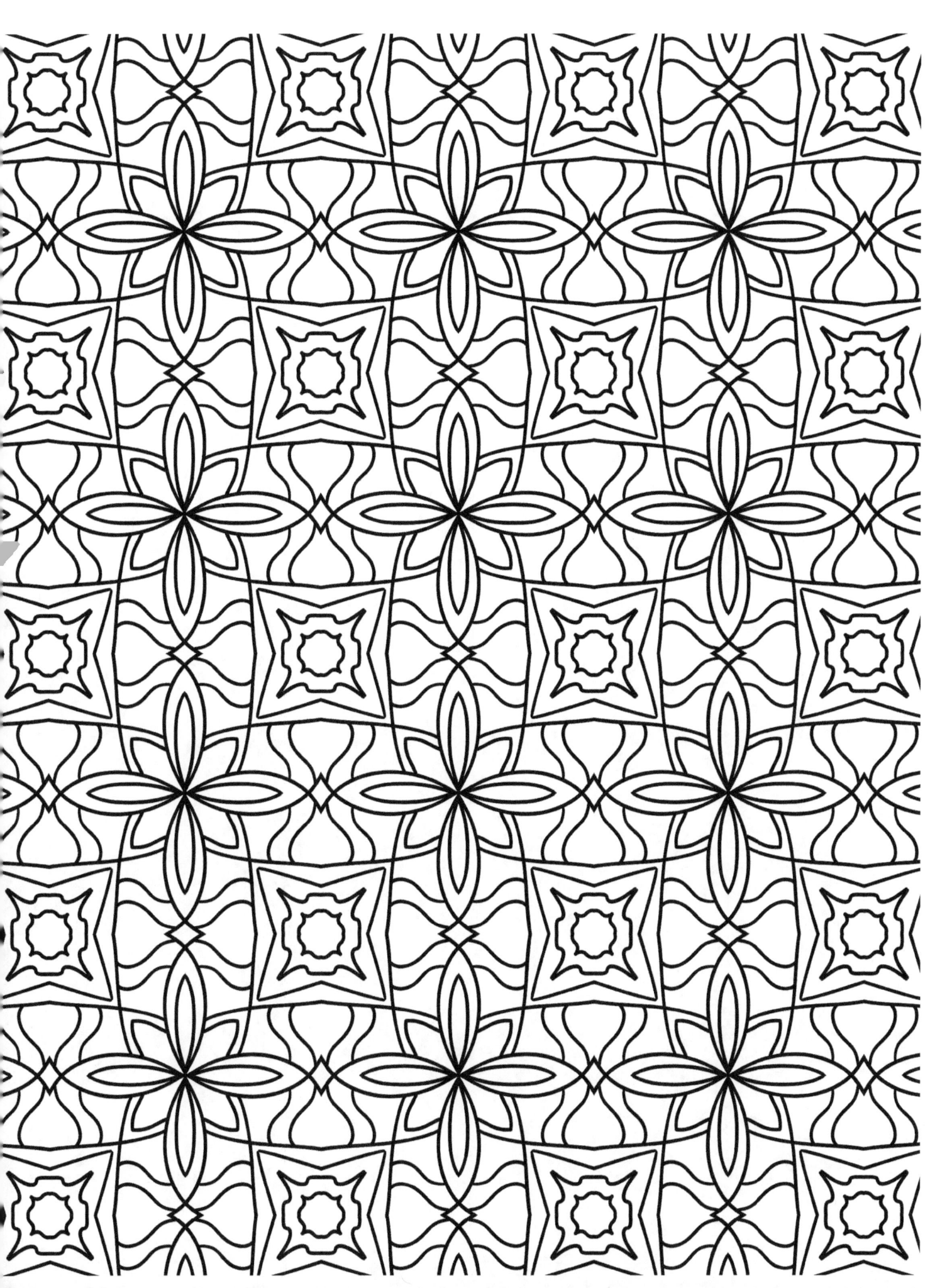

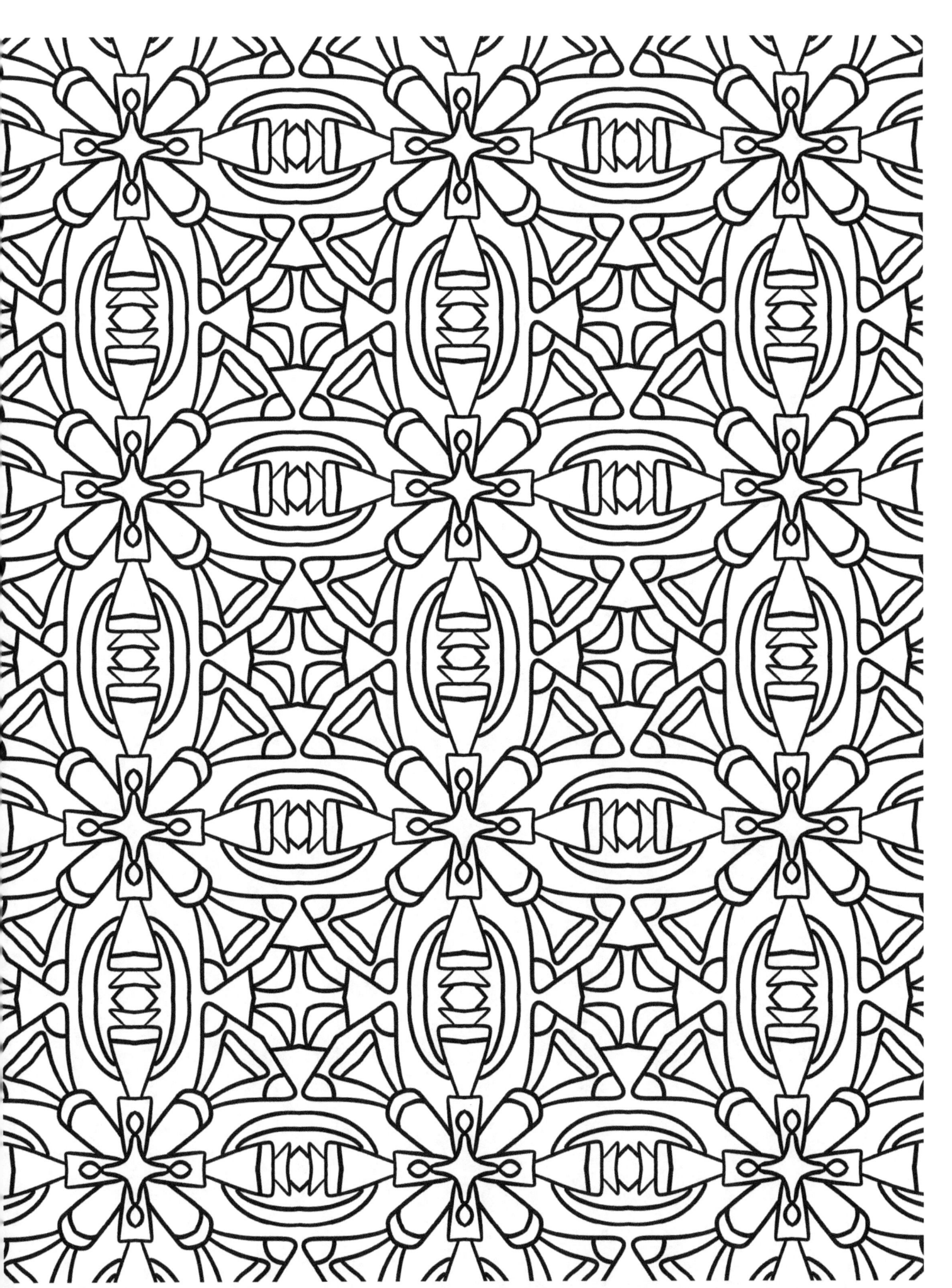

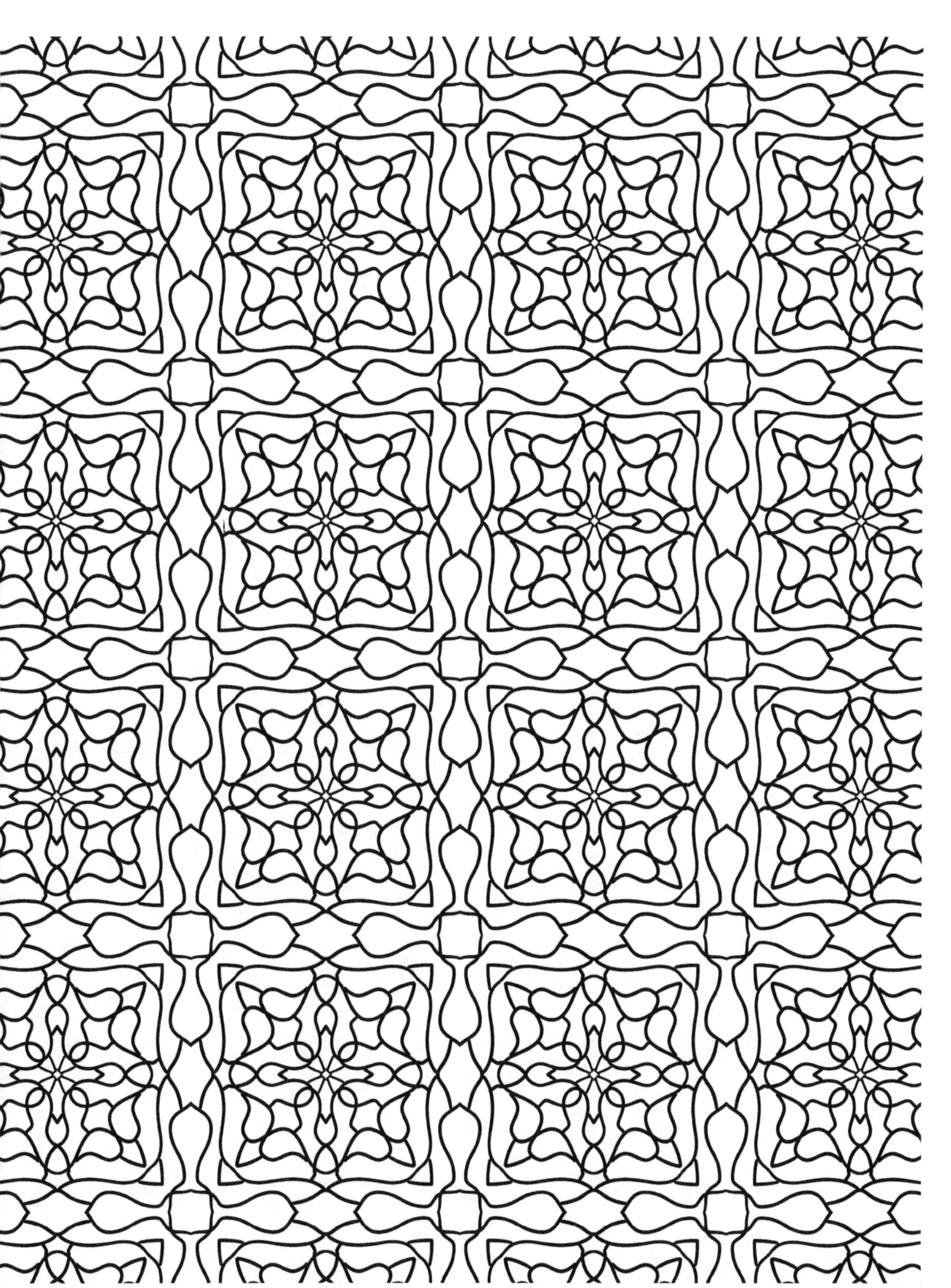

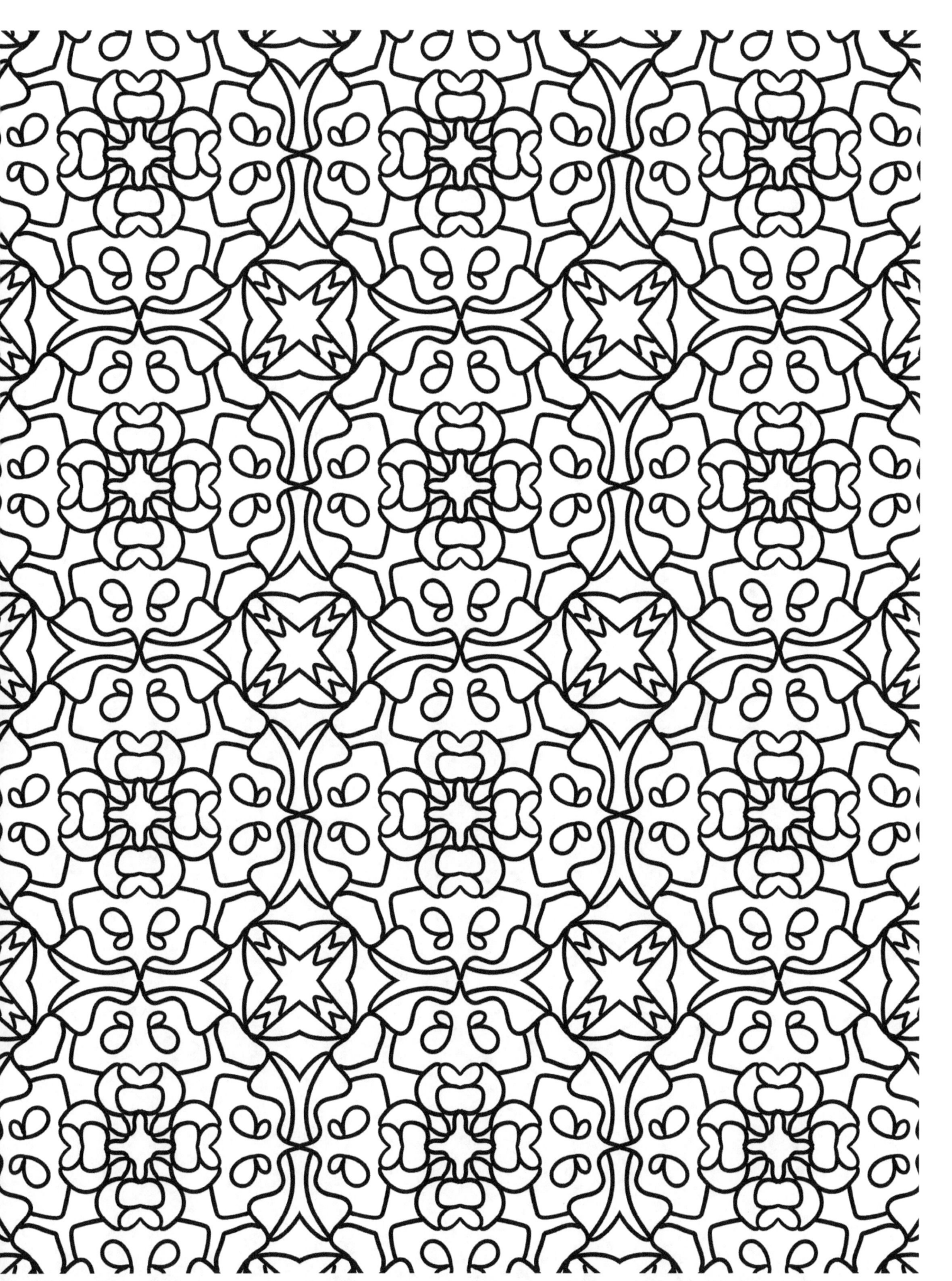

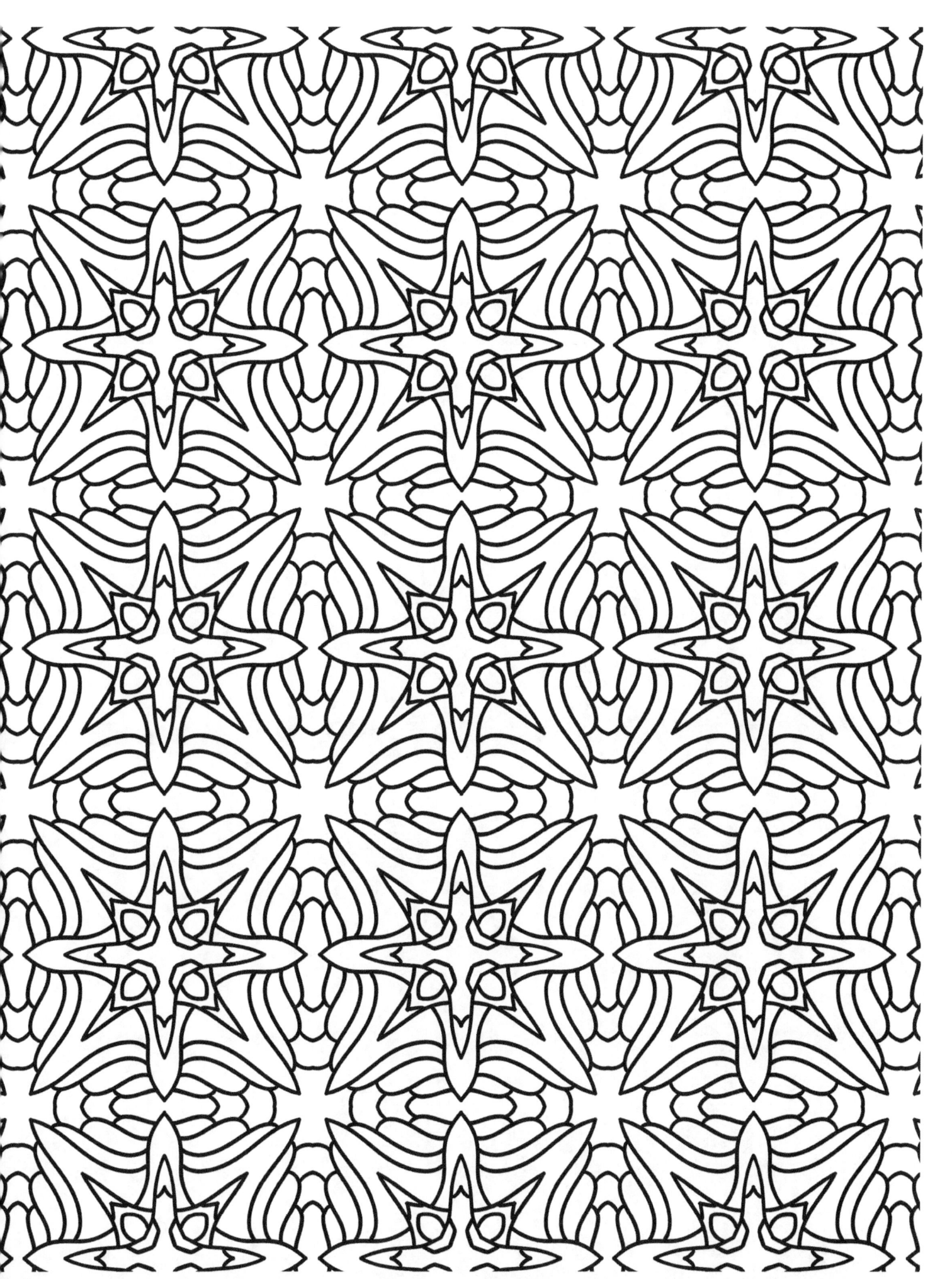

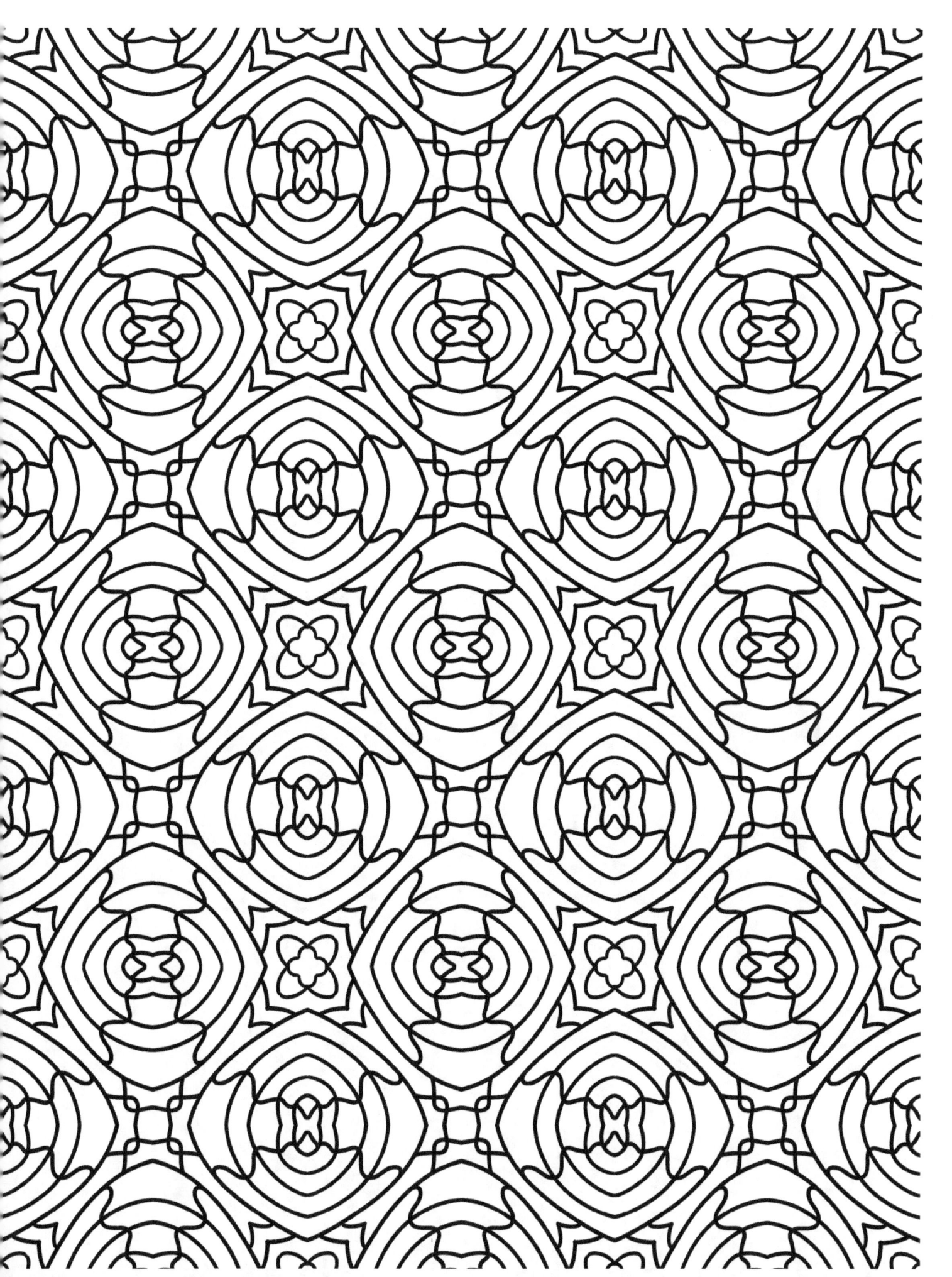

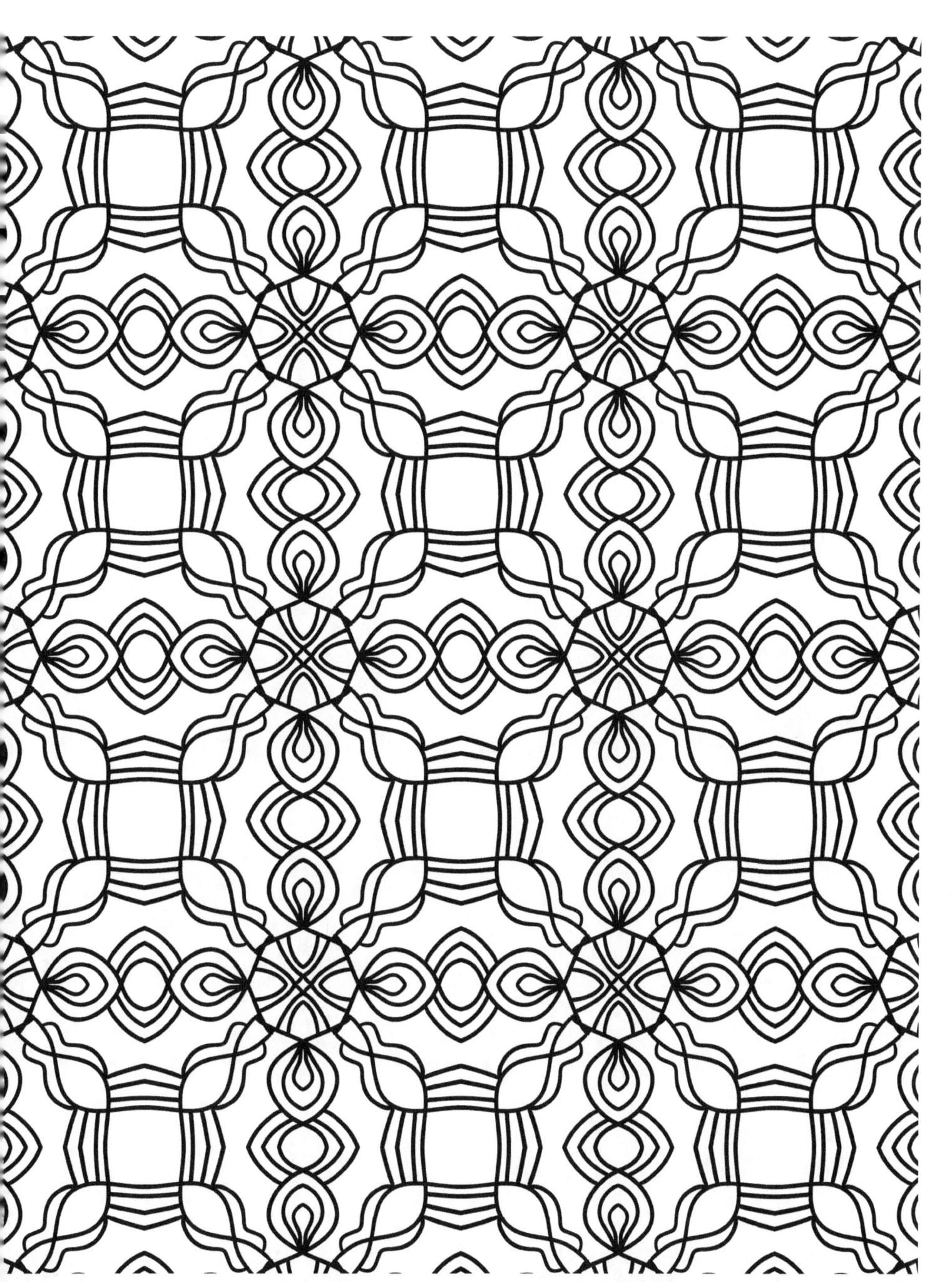

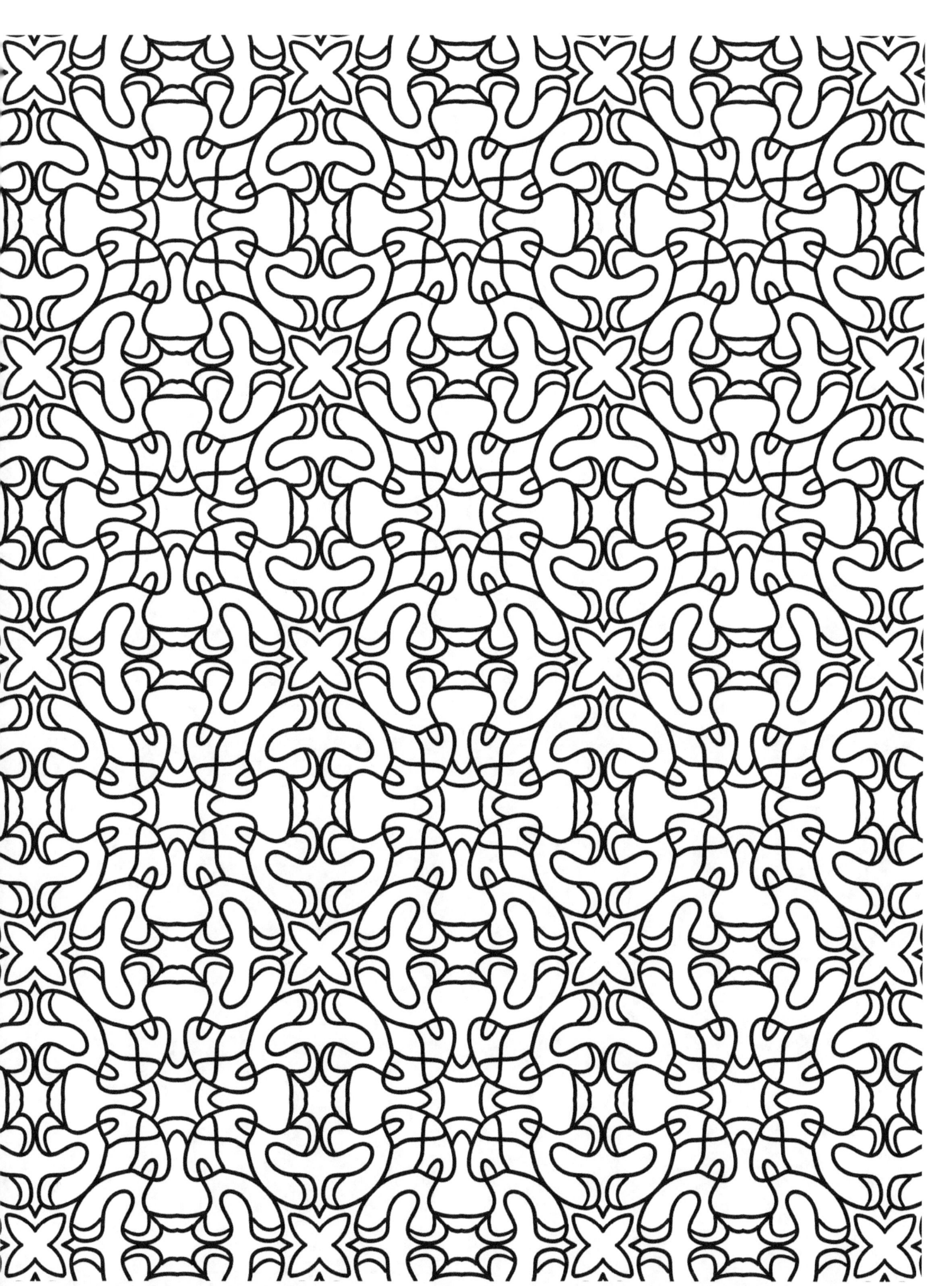

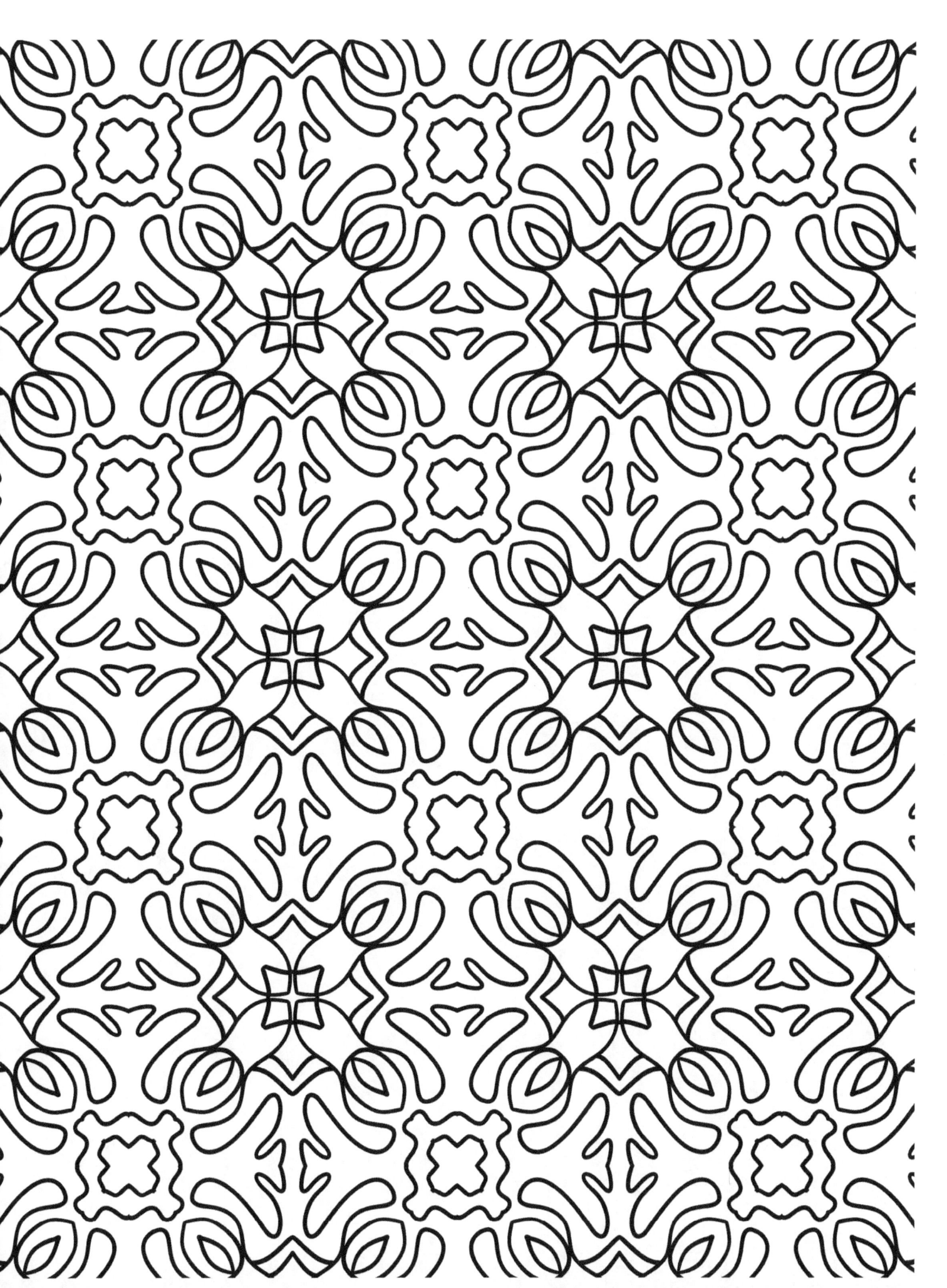

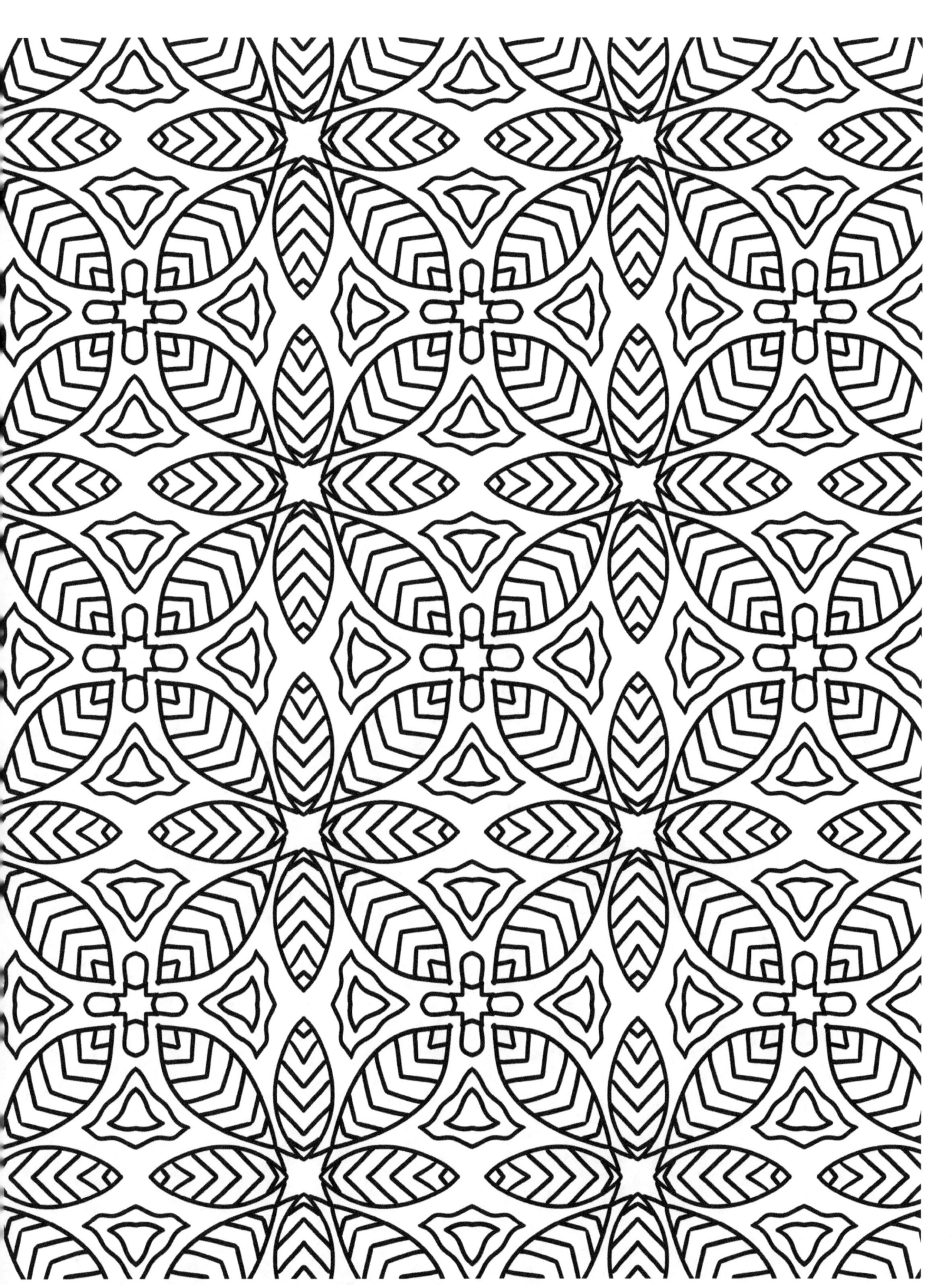

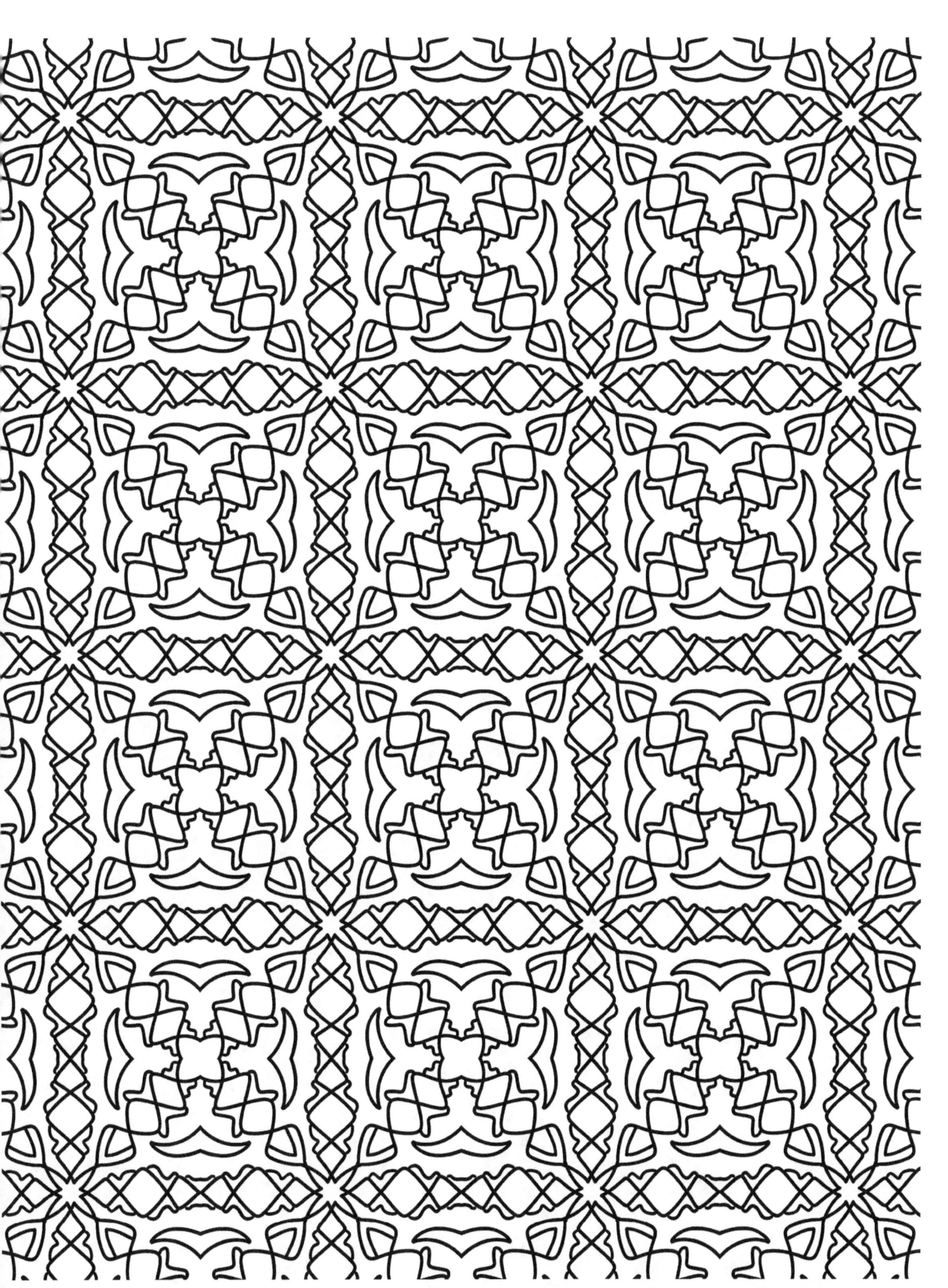

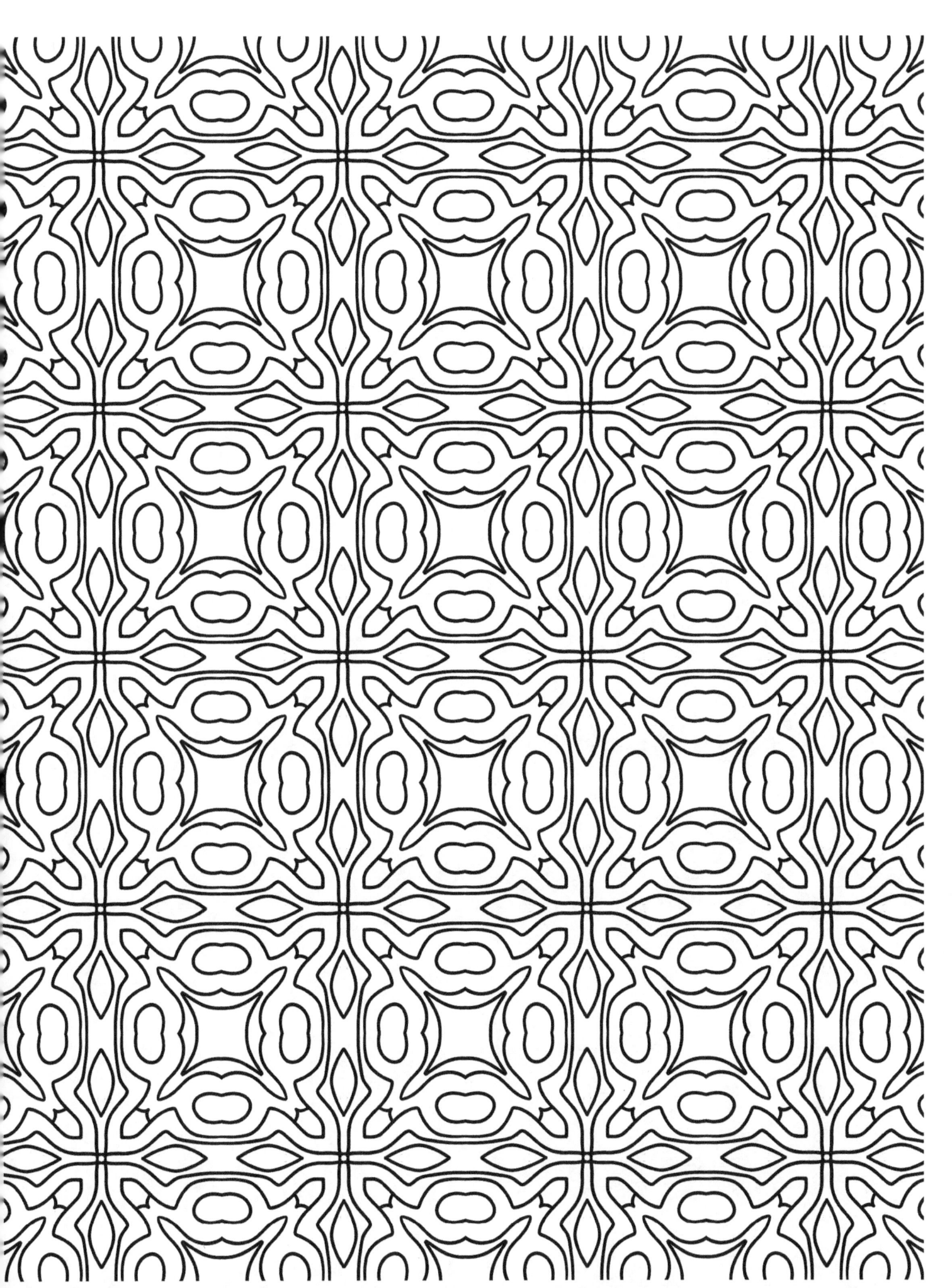

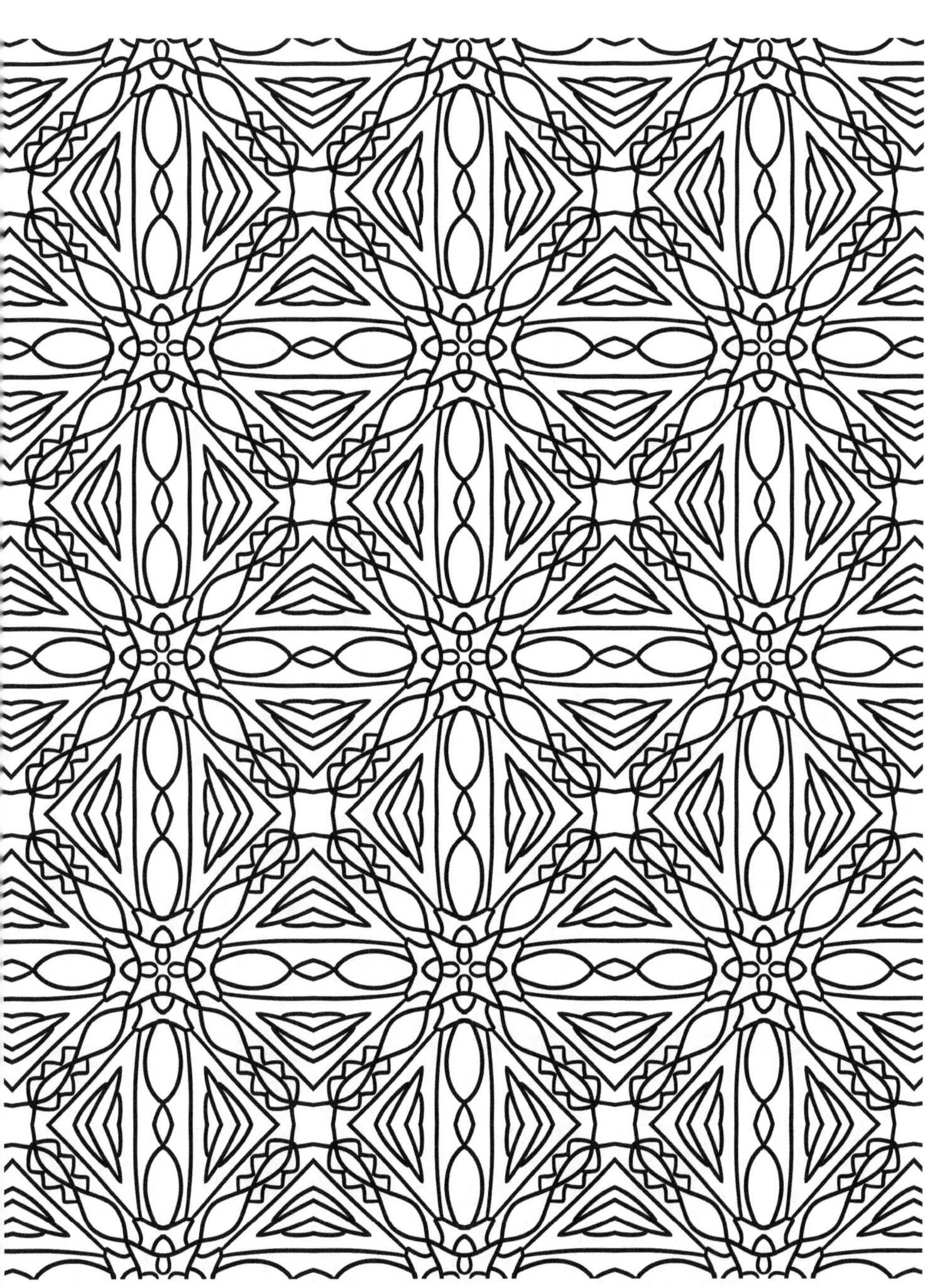

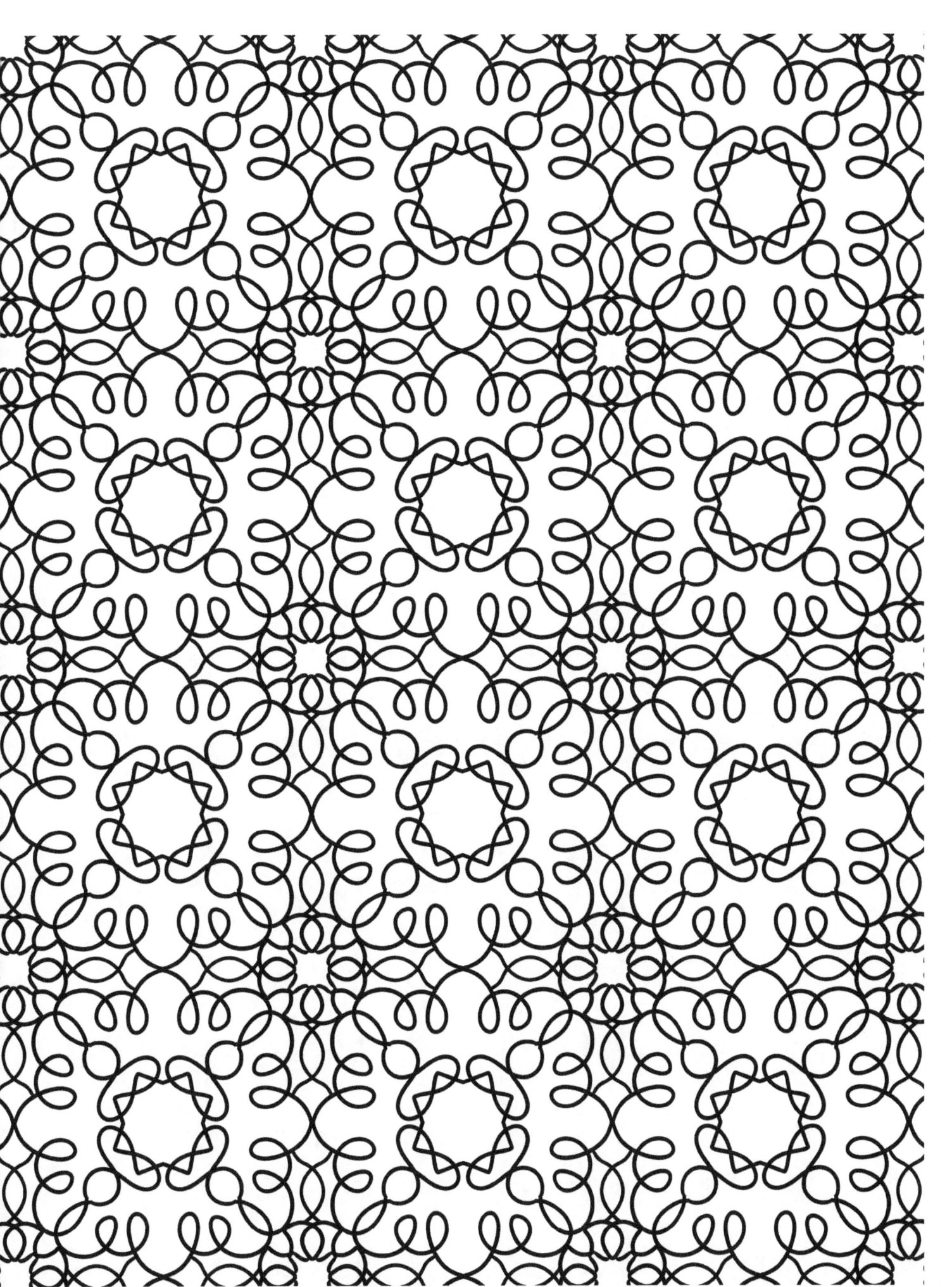

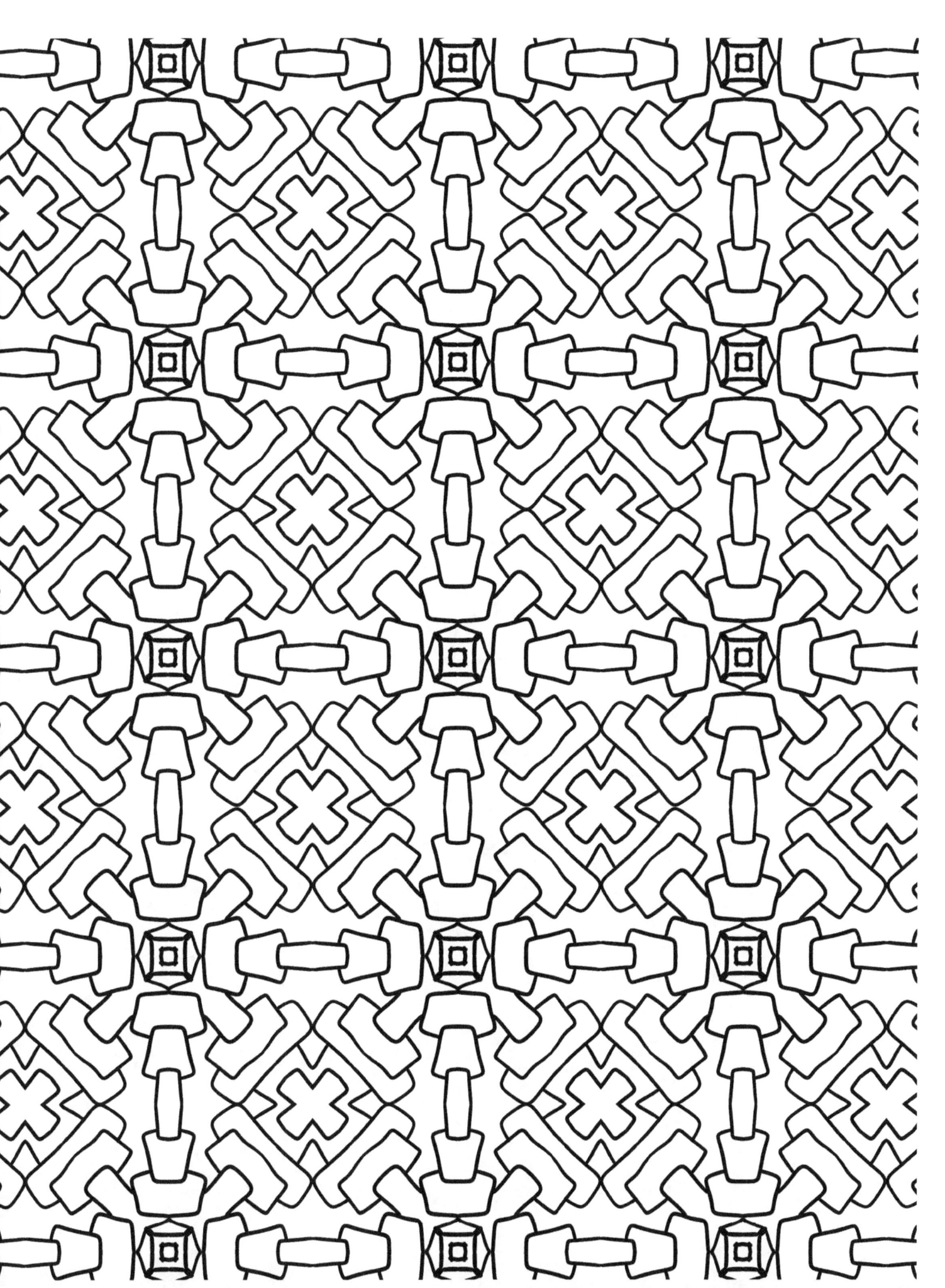

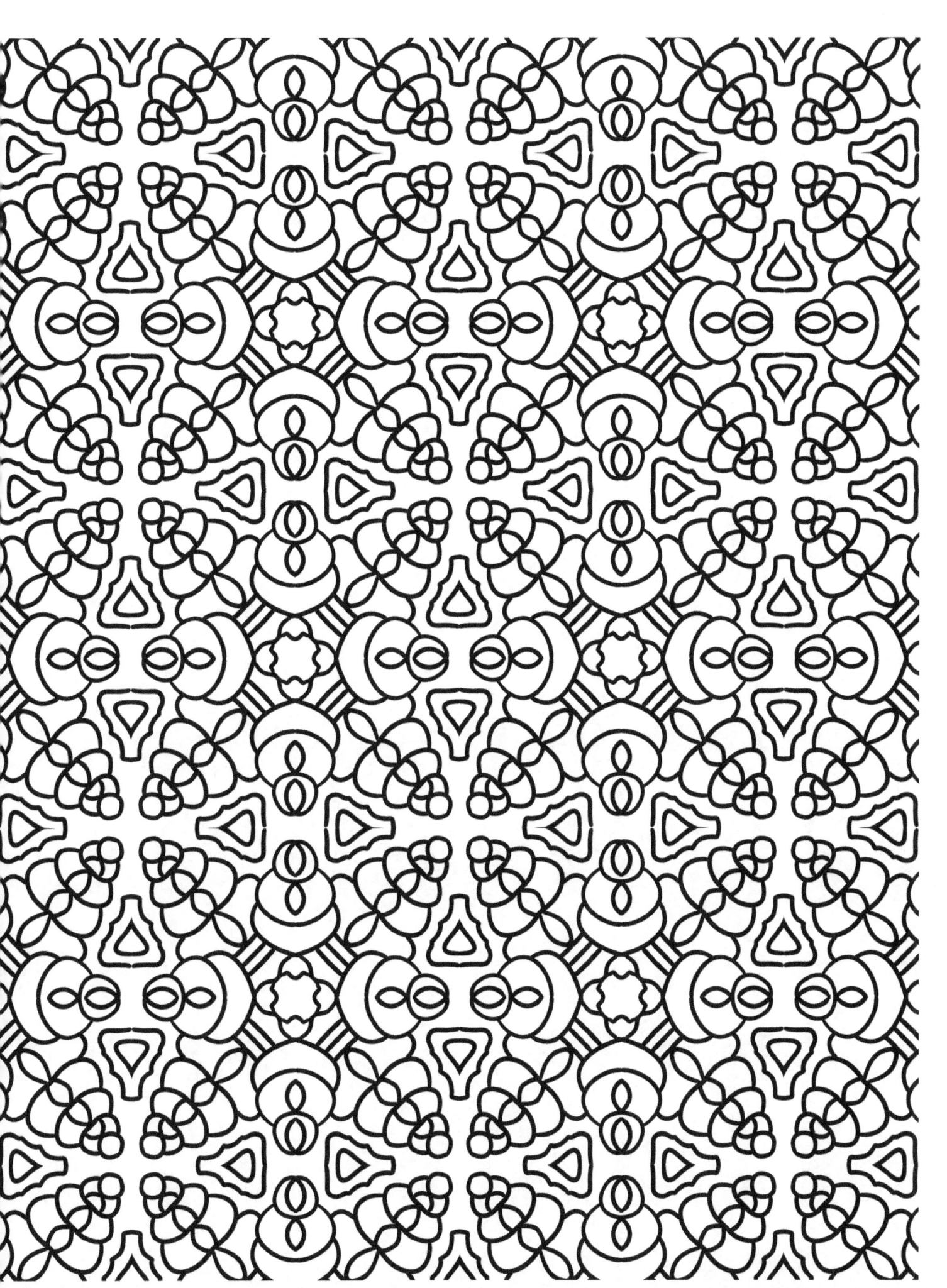

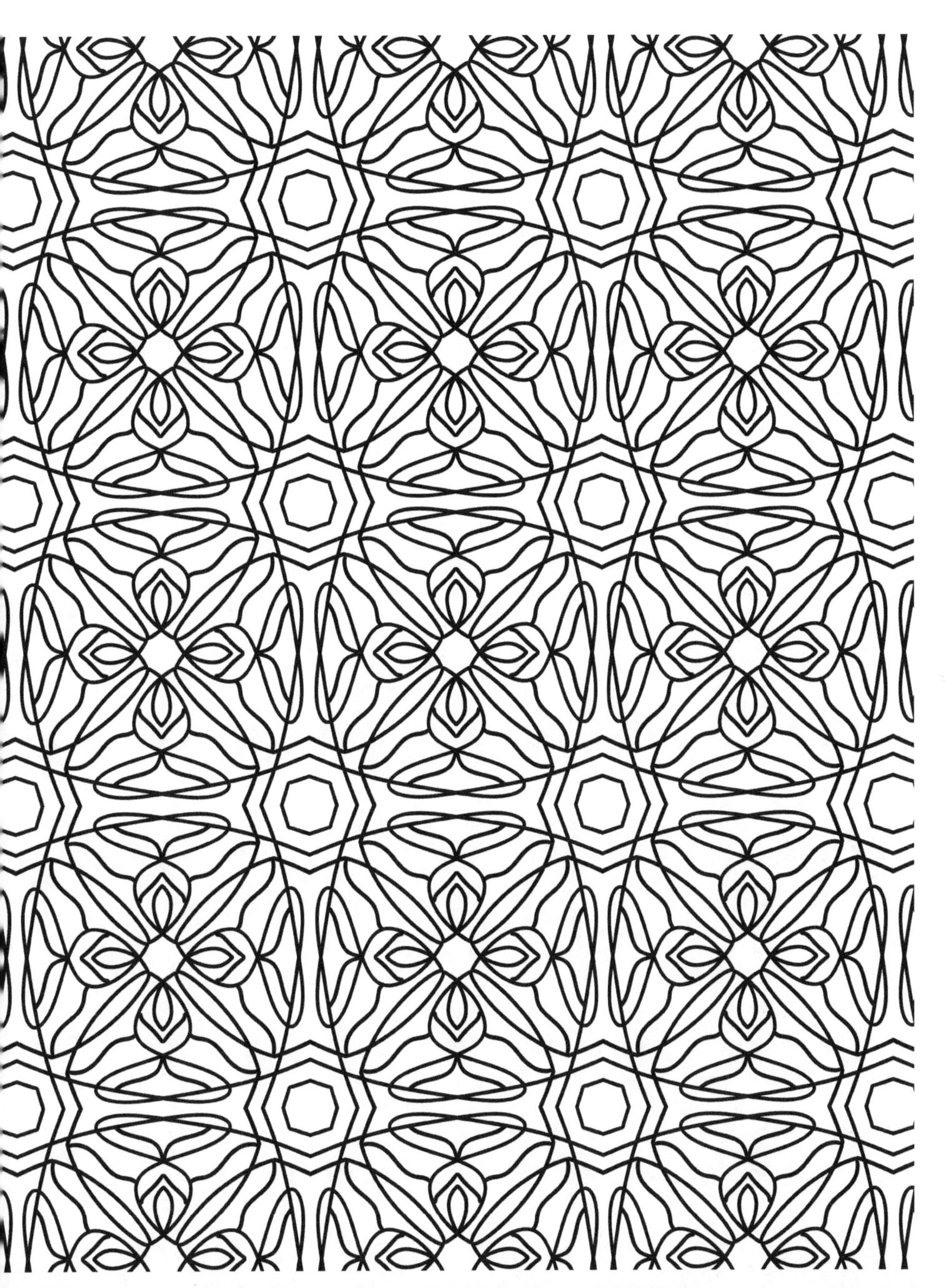

For more designs and upcoming books, please visit our
facebook group at :

@coloringbooksandmandalas

www.ingramcontent.com/pod-product-compliance
Lightning Source LLC
Chambersburg PA
CBHW080646180526
45168CB00008B/3326